The Truth About Dreams

Kelli Rae Hurst

I0224615

Scripture quotations are taken from the Holy Bible, New Living Translation, copyright ©1996, 2004, 2007, 2013, 2015 by Tyndale House Foundation. Used by permission of Tyndale House Publishers, Inc., Carol Stream, Illinois 60188. All rights reserved.

Scriptures taken from the Holy Bible, New International Version®, NIV®. Copyright © 1973, 1978, 1984, 2011 by Biblica, Inc.™ Used by permission of Zondervan. All rights reserved worldwide. www.zondervan.com The "NIV" and "New International Version" are trademarks registered in the United States Patent and Trademark Office by Biblica, Inc.™

Scripture quotations marked MSG are taken from *THE MESSAGE*, copyright © 1993, 1994, 1995, 1996, 2000, 2001, 2002 by Eugene H. Peterson. Used by permission of NavPress. All rights reserved. Represented by Tyndale House Publishers, Inc.

*Taken from The Message Translation of the Bible. All other scriptures cited are from the New International Version or New Living Translation.

Copyright © 2017 Armament

All Rights Reserved.

ISBN-13: 978-0692888476

ISBN-10: 0692888470

Vision Regarding My Father Following His Passing

DEDICATION

This book is dedicated to loving fathers and mothers—

those natural and spiritual.

In Loving Memory of:

George Ray Hensley

1955-2015

John Paul Jackson

1950-2015

PREFACE

In the first section of the Bible, the Old Testament (testament meaning *'agreement'* or *'covenant'* or even a *'solemn declaration of one's wishes'*) there is a phrase that is stated over and over again. The phrase varies but sounds something like this: "So that you may know that I am the Lord"; "Then you will know that I am the Lord who ..."; "So that you will see and know that I am the Lord"; "I am the Lord who ...". This phrase is in the Old Testament alone over 160 times. This fact tells us that God is preoccupied with our knowing who he is. He wants to show himself to us, for his *true* nature to be seen.

Then, in the New Testament, crowning this theme that builds in the Old Testament from this repeated phrase to God's constant interactions with man, Jesus comes to earth. Truly, the most profound way for God to ultimately reveal himself to mankind is to put himself in the form of a human—in tangible flesh and blood.

My desire, the desire of anyone who knows and loves God, is to also reveal who he is. Our very existence, DNA, and the created world in all its intricate beauty and majesty were intended to exemplify and magnify the character and wonder of our one, crazy-amazing God. I pray this book, if nothing else, does just that. I pray that we are willing, desiring and have the patience to receive what he wants to reveal. He is worthy of being known. He is worthy of being seen. He is worthy of being loved. He is worthy of our trust. He is worthy.

INTRODUCTION

The idea for this book came through a dream. A night vision, more specifically. I was on vacation. And, as often happens when I'm in another geographical region, I had a profound, spiritual, night experience. I saw a picture in my sleep of a book on dreams, its style, and layout. It woke me up in the dead of night, and I proceeded to lock myself in the bathroom for the next several hours, taking notes and meditating.

That was the conception of this book. It was an idea I knew didn't come from me. You know when something is outside the bounds of your natural capacity. I knew it was God; a God-bomb dropped in my spirit that carried the potential for rapid growth, great impact, and sudden expansion outside of what I could come up with myself. And, no surprise. That is exactly what dreams have been for me. It became increasingly clear that night, that is what he wants to share with everyone.

This project has not been merely an act of obedience.

My heart in making this book is to reveal the kind intentions of God the Father, which has the potential to be *greatly* manifested in our dream life. Despite the darkness and fear that are too often peoples experience with dreaming, they can receive vision of God's good desire for them, regularly. I want to share the profound impact that I have experienced through God-dreams in my own life, knowing that it is available to all.

But I must give a disclaimer here: I do not intend to give the impression that all dreams are from God. They are not. However, I firmly believe that many more ARE from him than what is conventionally thought. Furthermore, God is a redeemer, a recycler so to speak, and he is champion at taking the ugliest and darkest and turning it around for something good.

The nature of dreams is so complex and varied, no book will ever be able to address every potential principle and scenario that may manifest in them. God has a tendency to speak just outside of the bounds of our understanding in order to stretch us and cause us to reach toward him for answers. This books purpose is simply to lay a foundation from which we may build upon going forward. There are certain spirit principles that must be put in place, and then what may follow thereafter is up to the Crafter and the dreamers of dreams.

When announcing the imminent birth of the Messiah, the messengers (angels) proclaimed, "Peace, *goodwill* toward men." The Creator's will toward us is *good*. I can't describe how much I have found that to be abundantly evident through dreams.

Later, Jesus also said, "I will not leave you as orphans. I will *come to you*." Contrary to popular belief, he doesn't want to leave us alone to fall to the products of our own actions and devices. He wants to be involved in our process and potential. Dreams are a special and powerful vehicle he uses to do just that.

But like any other area or thing of great value, the enemy of our souls has fought our sleeping microcosm *hard*. He's fought it with terror, fear, confusion, and fallacy. We *must* take it back. What I desire to do through this book is illuminate a widely misunderstood subject that has been attacked, adulterated, and overcomplicated, and put it in terms of almost child-like purity and simplicity. My hope is to lay a fertile groundwork in which the Truth of this matter can take root and grow.

There are hearing exercises planted throughout. I dare you to try them. Learning how to commune and converse with the Dream-Giver is crucial for anyone who wants the fullness of what the experience of a dream is meant to illicit.

When we first begin thinking of God speaking to us, it is easy to think his voice will come in a way that is bold, obvious, and clear. The skies will open, the angels will sing, and it will be undeniably God. And God does speak obviously at times. But that line of thinking causes us to doubt that he will speak at all, believing such events rarely happen, and only to the 'chosen'. However, I have found that God speaks mostly in ways that require faith to hear, and often. We will recognize him proportionally to the degree we believe it's him speaking and not ourselves. There will always be reasons to doubt. We must choose the reasons to believe. We must believe he wants to speak to us, and will. His Word to us says that when you come to God, you must believe in him *and that he will reward you* for seeking him (Hebrews 11:6).

God only gives us measures of himself that we can handle at any given time. Without the ongoing regeneration of his Spirit, our finite beings are poor receptors for the infinite. After all, only spirit understands spirit. Too much of a great thing tends to overwhelm, disillusion or foster pride. If we are not ready for it, greater measures of this revealed understanding can make us unable to function practically in the ways that we need to for our daily lives and destinies. Therefore, it is important to grow in relationship with God, for as the relationship grows, so does our spirits capacity to receive him in fuller measures.

This book is centered around the theme that dreams are supernatural and spiritual in nature. Therefore, it is important to note that one cannot divorce dreams from the state of the spirit. We also cannot divorce matters of the body and soul from matters of the spirit. Despite what we often tell ourselves, our minds, hearts, bodies, and spirits are connected in such a way that one is always affected by the others. Whether it be fixations, mind-altering substances, falsehood, too much media, desires and appetites, etc., each affects *all* parts of us. So, what we continually feed ourselves, *metaphorically speaking*, will be made manifest in our dreams. If we want to have dreams that originate from us and feed our physical or emotional desires, we are sure to have them. Likewise, when we fix our eyes on God and allow him to take us through the process of cleaning out the negativity, things that take up valuable internal space, and hold us back from being who we are made to be, we will find that his voice becomes clearer in our dream life and with increasing frequency. And, our desires met after all, in a way that is fulfilling and long-lasting.

Dreams are like encrypted messages for our lives. The Bible is the key to unlocking the code. It tells us about Gods ways and personality, his likes and dislikes, approvals and disapprovals. His Spirit is the one who teaches us how to use the key correctly. If the key we're using isn't the right one or if we're using it incorrectly, the final message and conclusions will be incorrect or incomplete. We must use the Word of God as our foundation in seeking to interpret dreams and welcome the intimate friendship of the Holy Spirit. If we are spiritual beings and dreams are spiritual in nature, then it is *impossible* to get accurate interpretations without the help of the source of spiritual speech. Fortunately for us, God's Word has *a lot* to say on the subject and his Spirit is eager to help all who are willing to yield to his leading and preeminence.

Writing, drawing or in some way recording interactions are not required, but many people find that it helps them to express and process what they are seeing, hearing, feeling or sensing from God. His interactions with us do not necessarily come in the form of linear words or sentences. He can speak in pictures, feelings, senses and more. Documenting these communications put them in a form that our minds can more easily process. Additionally, there is encouragement and empowerment in being able to look back over what God has spoken to us. Capturing the moment also shows that we regard and appreciate the exchange, and what is valued and cultivated is rewarded and multiplied.

Throw your God-boxes out. Throw your assumptions out. Don't assume his communications to you should look or sound the way they do with others. And don't try to make something happen. Simply create space for him. Allow him to surprise you. Allow him to offend you. Allow him to love you. And believe that if you are willing to step toward him with even the tiniest bit of faith, he will not lead you astray. He wants to speak to you. He wants to show you things. First believe, then you will see.

I have been studying dream interpretation diligently for roughly three and half years. It hasn't come easy for me. I have studied, read, diagrammed and practiced, often for entire days at a time (God love my family) struggling to gain understanding of this special gift that I knew God was leading me into. I have had to fight for it. Somewhere along the way I realized that if it hadn't been a fight, I could have easily taken this profound and dazzling gift for granted.

While on this journey, I found that as much good, biblically-based and doctrinally sound information I had gathered, I was still at times just as unsure of my ability to interpret dreams as I was in the beginning. Regarding my level of maturity in being able to interpret dreams I felt I was in a perpetual stage of infancy.

Information does not necessarily equal progress in matters of a spiritual nature. I learned the hard way that spirit language is something better understood in the heart and in the imagination than in the intellect. It does not follow the rules of logic as we know them. Yes, we must have knowledge, but knowledge is there for the having. If you are willing to order a book, take a class, read an article or do a search on Google, you can find towering levels of information.

Revelation—an uncovering, a bringing to light, a revealing—from God is what we really need…what I really needed.

So, I sat down with my journal and pens as is my practice when I really need to hear something specific from God, and asked him this question:

"Heavenly Father, what is the truth about dreams?"

This book was his response.

"I, the Lord, reveal myself to them in visions, I speak to them in dreams."

-The Bible, Book of Numbers (12:6)

...his mind was troubled and he could not sleep. So the king summoned the magicians, enchanters, sorcerers and astrologers to tell him what he had dreamed...the astrologers answered the king, "May the king live forever! Tell your servants the dream, and we will interpret it." The king replied to the astrologers, "This is what I have firmly decided: If you do not tell me what my dream was and interpret it, I will have you cut into pieces and your houses turned into piles of rubble...So tell me the dream and interpret it for me."...

The astrologers answered the king, "There is no one on earth who can do what the king asks!...No one can reveal it to the king except the gods, and they do not live among humans." This made the king so angry and furious that he ordered the execution of all the wise men of Babylon. At this, Daniel went in to the king and asked for time, so that he might interpret the dream for him. Then Daniel returned to his house and explained the matter to his friends...He urged them to plead for mercy from the God of heaven concerning this mystery...During the night the mystery was revealed to Daniel in a vision. Then Daniel praised the God of heaven and said: "Praise be to the name of God for ever and ever; wisdom and power are his...He reveals deep and hidden things; he knows what lies in darkness, and light dwells with him...Take me to the king, and I will interpret his dream for him."

The king asked Daniel, "Are you able to tell me what I saw in my dream and interpret it?" Daniel replied, "No wise man, enchanter, magician or diviner can explain to the king the mystery he has asked about, but there is a God in heaven who reveals mysteries. He has shown King Nebuchadnezzar what will happen in days to come."

The Bible, Book of Daniel Chapter 2, New International Version

"A moment of insight from God is worth more than a lifetime of experience."

-John Paul Jackson

A CONNECTION with LIMITLESS POSSIBILITES

"Like lovers whispering words of affection in a sacred moment of confidentiality, dreams are intimate and powerful. They are one of my favorite ways to communicate with my most honored creation. They go straight to your heart or straight to your spirit. They bypass your doubts and inhibitions. It's only in waking that you are once again able to bring those negative factors into them. But that is not what I want for you.

Do you remember that dream I gave you where you were seeing two basins, one lesser and one greater? The lesser was 2-dimemsional and represented the soul—mind, will and emotions. The greater was multi-dimensional—dimensions you've yet to experience or know in your physical world—and represented the spirit.

The greater, or spirit basin, was full. The soul basin had only the *appearance* of being full. That is because the realm of the spirit will fill and satisfy you in ways that your mere mind, will and emotions can only do in part, and temporarily at that. The basin that was greater had an elephant coming out of it because elephants are literally *great*. True greatness comes through the spirit. When you are joined to me, we become "one" in spirit. You then have access to the very things I have access to and your spirit, which was once dead, is made alive. It is then that you are truly awakened to living a spiritual life. You are enlightened, and begin to grow.

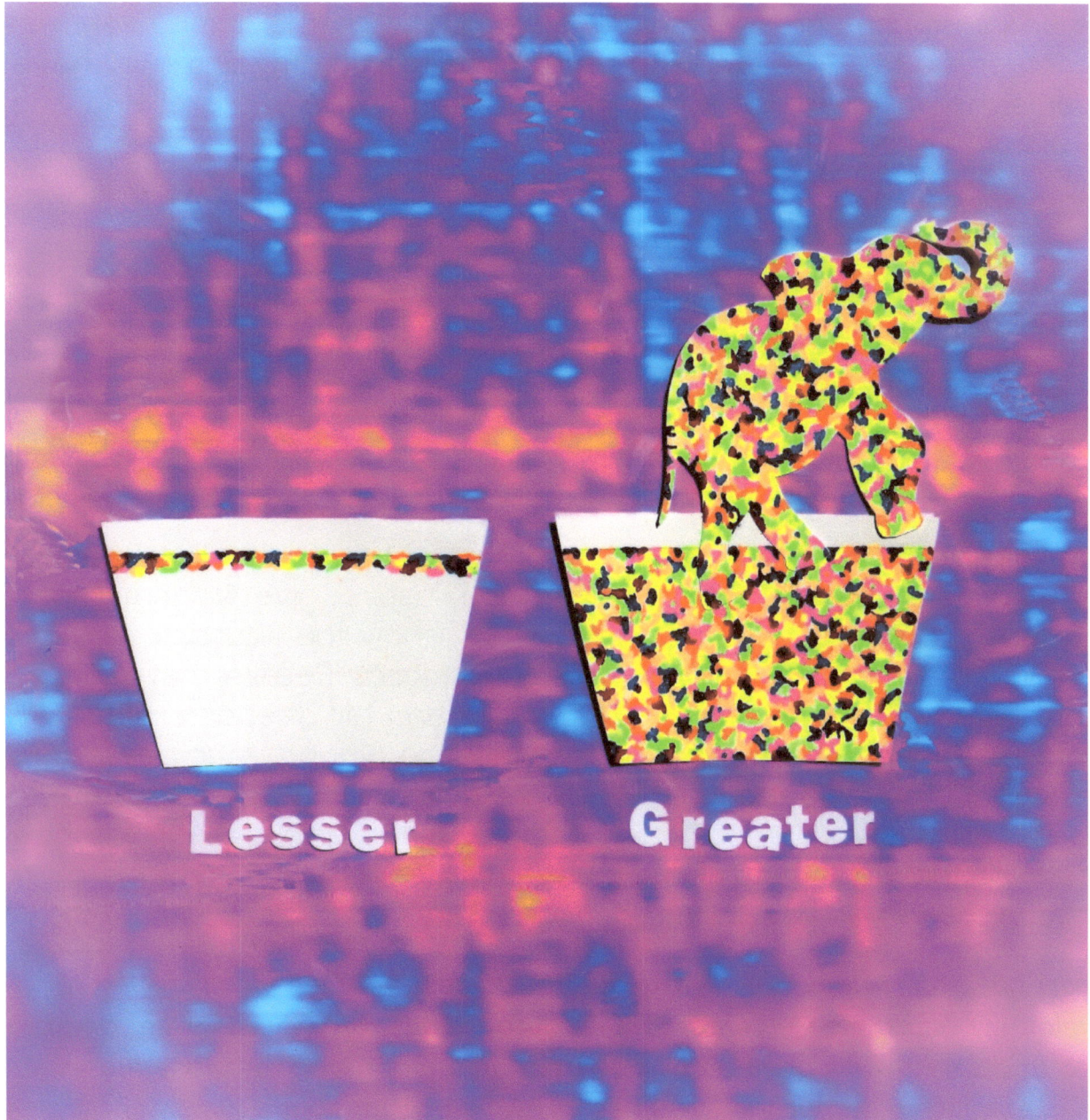

Lesser

Greater

"But the...Holy Spirit...will teach you all things..."

Like an infant growing in its mother's womb having the same dream as its mother, so you, growing and being connected in my Spirit will have dreams that my Spirit is having. Dreams about who you are, and about my plans for your future and destiny.

"When you are joined to me, we become "one" in spirit."

The purpose of this dream was to teach you a principle. But I have many purposes for dreams; to encourage, inspire, give wisdom, impart gifts, make promises, heal, reveal answers, show the future, lead you to pray about circumstances or people...and more. Realize that communications from me are multi-faceted and far deeper and more colorful than what you view as communication among your peers. You are limited by natural bounds. I am not limited. I can communicate to you in more ways than you can fathom. As you grow in learning how to recognize the ways I speak to you, you will experience methods of communication you didn't even know existed."

Dream Backstory: I had this dream during a time when I was really trying to develop my "spirit man". This dream encouraged me to continue in that and gave me a grid for how the spirit realm operated on a more superior plane than the soul. Learning to be spirit-led was becoming non-negotiable.

"I know the plans I have for you," says the Lord. "They are plans for good and not for disaster, to give you a future and a hope."

-The Bible, Book of Jeremiah (29:11)

DREAM: Vampires

I was observing real vampires immigrating to our country. I knew one significant reason why they were was for the improved abortion services we offered. The vampires were bringing their sacred objects and practices with them, which they would perform at night under cover of darkness. During the day, they looked like anyone else. You would never suspect that they were vampires, or even threatening. They desired to turn everyone else into vampires too.

Since I was only observing and not involved in this dream, it was not about me. This dream was meant to show me something that was happening in our country so that I could pray about it*. This dream was showing me that the evil practices our nation was embracing (*abortion*) had opened the door to more evils (*vampires*) coming here in a very covert and unsuspecting way, with the intention of multiplying (*making more vampires*).

* "I searched for a man among them who would repair the wall and stand in the gap before Me on behalf of the land so that I might not destroy it, but I found no one." -God, Book of Ezekiel☐ (22:30)

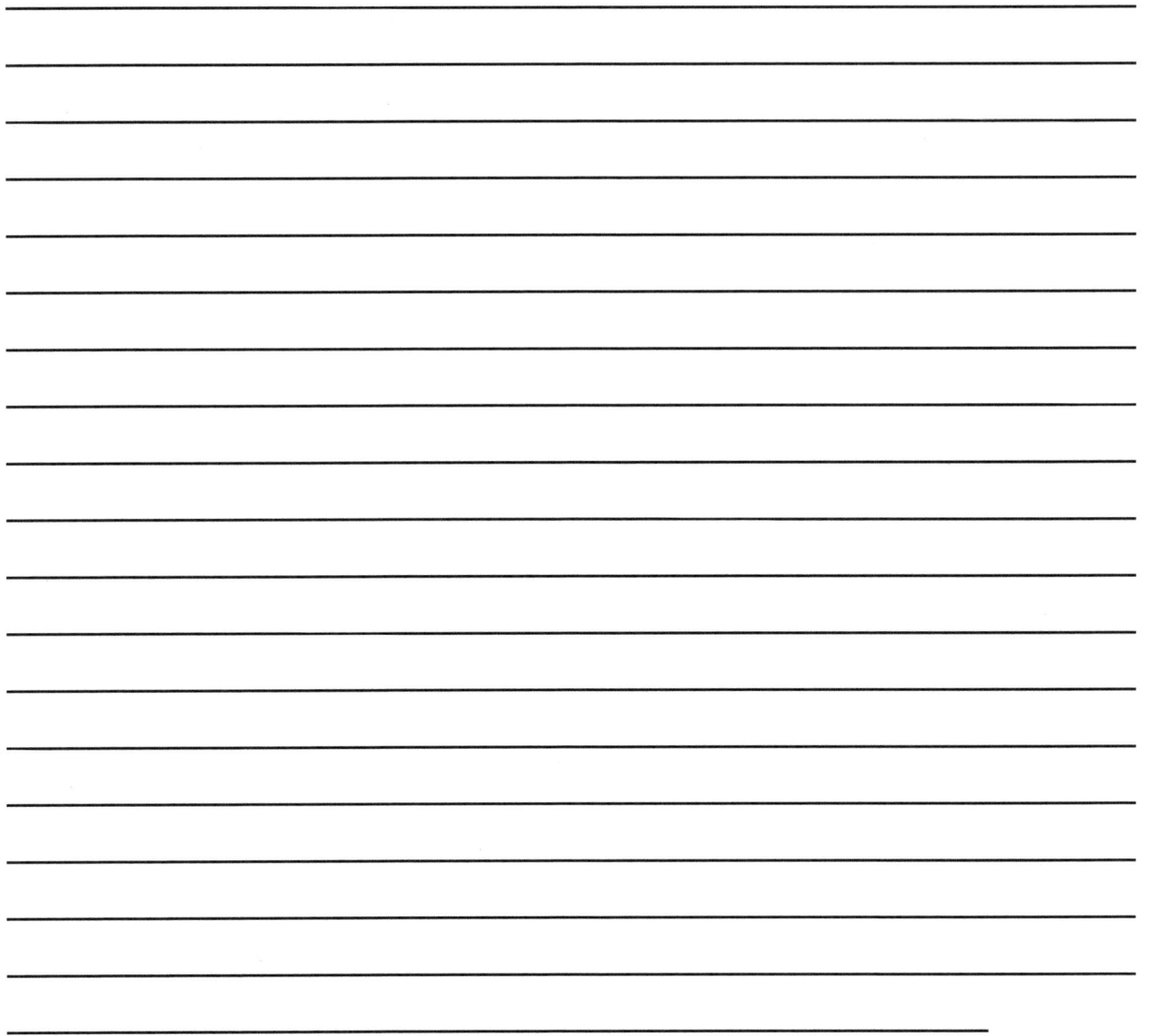

Find a quiet place, with a journal, sketchpad or voice recorder if you like. Ask God any question about any dream you've ever had. Or, if you can't remember one, any question about dreams in general. Record what you believe his response is.

"" ""

STRENGTH IN AN UNLIKELY PLACE

"Recall the dream you had where you saw three metal chair legs. The first leg was the strongest and it represented *children*. The second leg was a little weaker and it represented *adolescents*. The third leg was the weakest because it had a bend in it, representing *adults*. I told you this dream was about *childlike faith*.

Children do not believe that they already know everything. They realize they live in a vast, complex world, much bigger than them, that has yet to be explored. They experience something new every day. It is a form of humility. This makes them very strong spiritually. Adults, however, tend to be more aware of the things they know, as opposed to being open to all the things they don't, and that state of mind makes them weak spiritually.

"Whoever humbles himself like this child is greatest..."

I have more to show, teach, and give you than you have the capacity to ever receive in your short lifetimes. When you assume there is nothing new for you to gain from me at any given second you close yourself off from those things.

Furthermore, recognizing my hand and my voice in your life opens a new world of opportunities for you. The more you acknowledge what I am doing and value those things, the more I can justly do exponentially more for you because you are properly stewarding my presence and our relationship.

You see, I cannot continually go above and beyond for people who do not recognize that the source of all that goodness is me. If they believe those things come from anywhere else, that is what they will look to; that will be the fountain they visit. This would only lead them further away from me, and I couldn't, wouldn't, do that.

But, openness, willingness, and wonder before me, laced with expectancy, will open heaven's floodgates for you.

Dreams are a big way I pour out wisdom, protection and express my love. Just as I am infinite, so the ways I can speak to you, bless you and help you through dreaming are also infinite.

Yes, there is an aspect of dreams that require interpreting. I do this for many reasons. One, I only want those who are serious about hearing what I have to say to understand. I am called "The Word", right? I am always speaking to you, whether you perceive it or not. But that doesn't mean I will put precious things before people who will trample them like pearls in the mud. Would you reveal the longings of your heart to someone you knew wouldn't care very much? No, and neither do I. Concealing precious messages is a way that I can give, because giving is who I am, but it is up to the receiver of that message to decide whether they will open it or not. I will not give it fully opened, only to potentially deepen the rejection.

"I am always speaking to you, whether you perceive it or not."

Another reason I conceal messages is that I want my children to seek me, to ask me questions. The concealed nature of dreams pushes you toward me.

But the things I reveal are usually concealed anyway. Realize that I show you things because you don't see them yourself: things about you, about situations, about the future. I want you to be aware and have understanding. However, I will not give you all the answers and allow you to walk away having received what you wanted, and I not getting what I want, what I sent my Son to die for...you. That is like a prostitutional arrangement and I love you too much, am too committed to you, am too jealous for you, to settle for a transaction over a relationship.

Not only that, I am a just judge. I must, by my very nature, hold you accountable for what you know. 'To whom much is given, much is required.' If I were to give you great revelation, without the proportionally developed character to go with it, then I would be putting you in a dangerous and vulnerable position. And because I am kind and just, I will not do that."

Dream Backstory: When I had the dream about the chair legs it was around the time God was teaching me about the importance of childlike faith. I read stories about supernatural miracles children were experiencing in other parts of the world, and it totally transformed my thinking. It was HUGE. I had always struggled to hear God because I made it so much more complicated than it was. As we adults tend to do with everything. But that is not Gods way. Pure, simple faith like that of a child who knows they are loved is one of the most potent forces on earth. Understanding that significance and feeling the impact of it on my spiritual muscle unexpectedly changed my life.

It is God's privilege to conceal things
and the king's privilege to discover them.

-*The Bible, Book of Proverbs (25:2)*

DREAM: Kid Chopping Off Arm

I was doing volunteer work in a city for a group of young people with developmental and intellectual disabilities. These kids continually came up to me asking me to give them things and to do various petty tasks for them over and over, and they were hostile and demanding about it. There was one boy in a wheelchair, who had gotten the idea to cut the lower part of his arm off—so he did. He had developed some sick fixation with me and started following me around with a large knife thinking he would attack and chop my arm off too. I was constantly having to look over my shoulder to guard against him. I couldn't do anything I was supposed to do because of the distraction of this boy wanting to "improve" me.

What God was revealing through this dream was a picture of what was happening in my life at the time. I thought I was really accomplishing something by diligently tending to my bottomless to-do list. But this dream was a picture of what was happening behind the cloak of the physical world.

Dark forces were influencing me to focus on endless minute tasks (*continual petty requests*) in order to overwhelm, distract (*always looking over my shoulder*) and 'disarm' me (*chop off my arm*) from doing the things that were truly important (*volunteer work*) like focusing on people.

This dream was dark and creepy. It was not only revealing a strategy of darkness being used against me, but also how I was allowing it.

I was given this dream so that I would 1) recognize these personal tendencies as something my spiritual enemy wanted to weaponize against me, and 2) turn from my actions that allowed those plans to manifest.

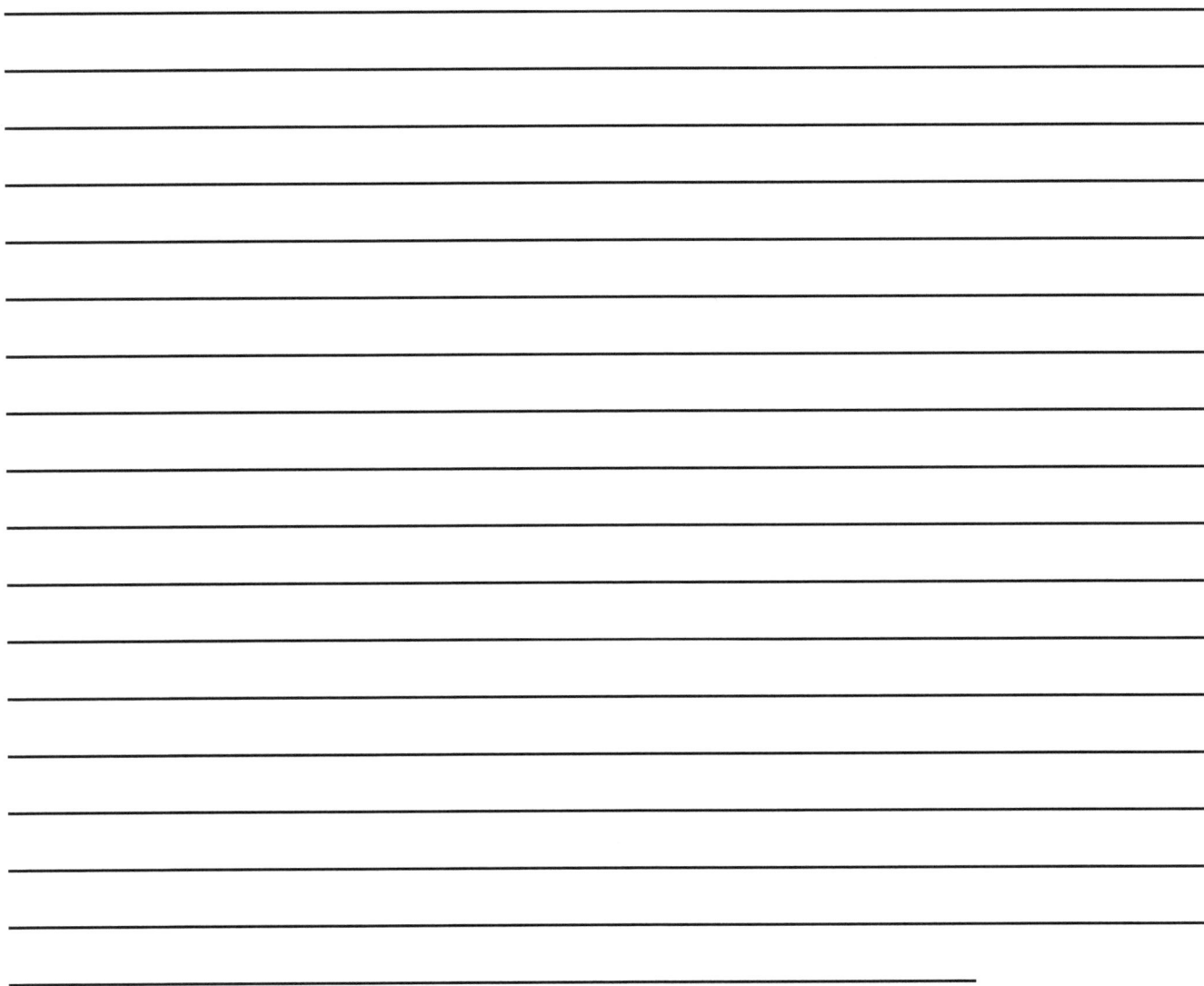

Ask God to bring to your mind something—a situation, person, experience, or issue you don't like. Ask him to show you how he sees that person or thing. Does his response alter or change your perspective or confirm it? What does his response tell you about his nature or character?

"" ""

WIRED FOR PICTURES

"The closer your heart is to mine, the clearer your dreams will be. The more your spirit is aligned with my Spirit, the more dreams you will have from the realm of light—from me.

Yes, there are dreams from yourself—'dreams you cause to be dreamed', and dreams from the realm of darkness that also occur. But even through those dreams I can easily show you things that are beneficial to you. I can turn what was meant for evil and use it for good. How will you do that without me? Can you see what I see?

I do love dreams for another reason—they are so effective! If a picture is worth a thousand words, how many words do you think a dream is worth? Depending on the dream, it could be infinite! And I love to dive the depths of those things with you.

"If a picture is worth a thousand words, how many words do you think a dream is worth?"

Think back to the dream you had where you were living in a house where there was a trickle of water flowing through it to the backyard. The trickle kept growing and growing until it was a flow that covered the entire kitchen floor. You were bothered by that, remember? Not only that, but it seemed to be alive, to have a mind of its own.

Then, your father and brother, whose faces you never saw, were carrying crates of rotting fruit out of your house and putting them in a tree in your backyard. You also instinctively felt that someone somewhere was mad about it, although you never saw them. That was an awesome dream, wasn't it?! It was so exciting for both of us! Remember at the end when you were putting different hats on those white, styrofoam mannequin heads that were also sitting in a tree?

This dream is a beautiful example of the type of language used in dreams—picture language. Not just picture language, though. *Metaphoric* picture language. I could use literal picture language, and occasionally do, but that wouldn't require much imagination, would it? And I love imagination! I speak to you through it all the time (though you tend to think it's you. *Oneness*, remember?).

I also love metaphor and symbolism. These vehicles of communication provide so much depth, flexibility and creativity to be tapped into. I am called "The Creator" for more than just making the universe, you know.

Dream During a Blood Moon

In that dream, look at the fruit. Fruit is a general symbol for what is *produced* by your life. I say *your* life because this was your own house in the dream. No one else lived there, so this dream was about you individually.

The fruit was bad. You weren't producing many good things at that time in your life; things like love, joy and peace. Your father and brother, whose faces you never saw but knew weren't your natural father and brother, were taking care of it for you. It didn't take you long to figure out who they were, did it? I, your Father, and my Son, Jesus, were removing these negative issues.

How? By putting them on a tree. What was the tree in this case? Another name for 'The Cross' is 'The Tree'.

My Son, Jesus, paid the highest price for the greatest debt of sin when he allowed his blood, or *life*, to be expelled from his body through crucifixion. That blood flowed from him, into the ground, cleansing this world, and bearing the immense weight of your issues for you.

As it was shown in the dream, it all simply came down to allowing us to dispose of those issues for you (you knew this tree represented the cross and not one of the many other possible meanings for 'tree' because of the context it was in. And it just "clicked" inside of you that the meaning was right).

You knew instinctively that someone somewhere was not happy about this taking place. You didn't see him in the dream because his involvement was *inconsequential* (hint—Jesus stripped him of his authority in Hades after being crucified).

The water part of the dream, the water that seemed alive, was extra special. I speak to you and others often out of my Word, the Bible, so it is so important that you know it. Read it with me. Ask me to show you hidden mysteries in it, even if you are reading parts you think you already understand or could have no application to you at all. There are limitless layers of understanding beneath the surface. I love to reveal these things to you, so don't be satisfied to read them at surface-level.

The rulers of darkness can and will come masquerading as beings of light, trying to trick and deceive those who are vulnerable. Knowing my Words, and my ways in them, not only make you a smaller target, but gives you a standard by which to measure every spiritual experience (for I never do anything to violate my own Word). It also makes it easier for my Spirit to teach and show you things. It's better to be taught through the grid of truth that you already know.

"Knowing my Words, and my ways in them, give you a standard by which to measure every spiritual experience."

For instance, you know that one name or symbol for my Spirit in the Scriptures is "Living Water". When you saw that element in the dream, you picked up on it immediately. You then understood that this dream was me telling you that Holy Spirit was going to begin to flow through your life (*house*) in increasing measure (although you didn't always find it pleasant to not be in control—thus, your discomfort over it).

You understood this. You also understood that there were negative things we were going to rid from your life through the overcoming power of the Cross of Jesus.

What you didn't understand was why you were putting hats on the mannequin heads. I didn't reveal that part because the time wasn't right. Timing is so important. I alone hold time in my hand. I know when to reveal what you need to know in a way that is going to most protect you and benefit you and others.

But, there's also the point that, because of your frame of mind, you wouldn't have received what it meant at the time anyway. You had a hard time believing anything positive about yourself or future. If I had told you then that this part of the dream meant *clarifying purpose for those lacking identity*, you would not have believed it. The lies you didn't even realize you were agreeing with by believing them were hindering your ability to get the full interpretation."

Dream Backstory: The dream about the bad fruit was very special to me because of the events surrounding it. That night, immediately preceding this dream, I was woken up by a voice calling my name. I heard it two or three times. I knew it was God, and this was the closest I had ever come to audibly hearing his voice. There's nothing like it, and it is a game-changer.

As it is meant to be.

This dream occurred on a "blood moon" night, which further reinforced the spiritual significance of it for me. This entire event was not only designed to give me a glimpse into Gods kind intentions for me. It also showed me beyond the shadow of a doubt that he saw me and loved me. It became clearer how personal, purposeful, and attentive he really was. Which was necessary in that I was soon to go through one of the hardest years of my life.

Everything written in the Scriptures was written to teach us.

-The Bible, Book of Romans (15:4)

The word of God is alive and active...

-The Bible, Book of Hebrews (4:12)

DREAM: Dress Shopping for a Wedding

I was in a women's clothing shop with several other girls. We were shopping for something to wear for a wedding. The store employees were helping us, but none of the dresses were formal. They were all casual, day-to-day dresses.

This dream was short, but rich with meaning. Since this dream was myself along with others involved in the action, I knew it was not just about myself, but applicable to others as well.

A woman or group of women can represent the church in dreams because the Bible refers to the church as *The Bride of Christ*. The wedding referenced was referring to the second coming of Jesus and his joining with his church. This is one possible meaning for weddings in dreams, and that meaning fit the context in this dream. We were preparing ourselves for Christ's return, and that's what the dress shopping was about.

It was revealed to me by Holy Spirit that this dream was saying, "You will not find the noble things you need to put on among the common." Then, I remembered this verse:

"In a wealthy home some utensils are made of gold and silver, and some are made of wood and clay. The expensive utensils are used for special occasions, and the cheap ones are for everyday use. If you keep yourself pure, you will be a special utensil for honorable use. Your life will be clean, and you will be ready for the Master to use you for every good work." (2 Timothy 2:20-21).

This verse not only contains a solid example of metaphor, it was also the core message of the dream: to make sure I am clean of dishonorable living and I will be positioned to be used for purposes of honor. Clothing symbolizes what we 'wear' in life, what we cover ourselves with; it describes aspects of ourselves. I wasn't going to be able to cover myself with noble things like truth, love, honor, purpose, etc. by doing the same old same.

I needed to separate myself from some dishonorable things like negative thought processes, embracing lies, lifeless activities, and things that gobbled up time and internal space. Instead, I needed to look in the place where noble things are found...alone time with God— loving him and allowing him to love *me*, prayer and meditation, reading God's Word, and serving people.

Ask God to show you a lie you are believing. It may be about him, you, someone else, a situation, an issue or an event. Then ask him to show you the truth. It may be as simple as shifting your focus away from one thing and realizing the right thing to focus on in its place.

A Word on Nightmares and Night Terrors

I understand fear. I know it well. I dealt with regular, overt intrusions and threats from dark spiritual forces until I was almost 30 years old. Through a profound, climactic night experience, all of that changed in an instant. But, I had to stand firm in my new freedom and not allow that evil presence to prevail when it tried to rear its insidious head again.

I have since found that unless we are somehow intentionally inviting evil and fear in, it is a very simple thing to deal with.

The attacks I experience were in no way invited. They came like a violation. One night, they reached a point where his just nature drove God to say, "No more", and he swept in like an assassin, swiftly and violently plucking away my foe like so much as a wisp of lint.

I gained priceless treasures of spiritual insight following that experience. I now see there are many tools for us to utilize when it comes to interacting in the unseen, but I think they can all be simplified into one message. When it comes to walking in spiritual peace and freedom over fear, there is one core fundamental that must be understood. This core fundamental is *agreement*.

Fear is the inverse of faith, which essentially says that I agree with God; I agree with what *God* says. When the spirit of fear comes, he is trying to get you to agree with *him*; with what *fear* says. And fear is always going to say the opposite of God.

If you choose to agree with what fear says—that it has power in your life, that it can harm you, that what it wants you to believe is true—then you have given it authority for those things to be so. Authority comes through agreement. This is a very important spiritual principle.

Not only do we need to make decisions and choose thought patterns in our waking life that demonstrate we are agreeing with God who is light, we need to disagree with the spiritual enemy when he tries to intrude into our lives, thoughts, and dreams. And you cannot agree with God and agree with enemy simultaneously. One is truth, and the other false.

Practically speaking, as far as the spirit of fear thinks he can get you to agree with him, he will go. We must show him that no matter his tactics, we are sure in our agreement with God, and darkness is not getting anywhere with us. Fear may be a dictator, but we are not his subjects.

Nightmares do happen, and they are allowed by God only to show the enemy's hand and to train us in how to fight. God wants you to know his strategy so you can *forbid and disagree* with it. It will always be a lie.

We do not agree with lies. We do not believe threats. We do not put our faith in fear, and therefore empower it. We believe truth. We trust in the power of God to uphold and protect us. We agree with the promises entrusted to us by God in his Word. We will *know* the truth, and it will set us free.

"My son, do not let wisdom and understanding out of your sight, preserve sound judgment and discretion; they will be life for you...When you lie down, you will not be afraid; when you lie down, your sleep will be sweet."
-The Bible, Book of Proverbs (3:21-24)

DON'T DISCARD THE SCRAPS

"One very important thing to keep in mind about dreams, in contrast to the fruit dream, is that they are not always so obviously spiritual. In fact, I whisper more than I shout. You really must listen. If you truly value what I am saying, you will value *all* your dreams and not just the ones that stick with you throughout the day. Even if you only remember fragments.

When you are interpreting dreams, it can be easy to get thrown off by the ones that have multiple scenes. It may help you to interpret each scene individually, then put them together. If you only remember one or two scenes, those scenes can still have meaning on their own. Don't discard them. Even if they seem strange.

"I whisper more than I shout."

Like that night when you dreamed that two packs of butter cost $39.99. That was the only thing you could remember out of what seemed to be an entire night of dreams. It seemed silly and random, but you valued it anyway. And it turned out to have meaning for you, didn't it?

You knew butter, which is a form of fat, was an ancient symbol for prosperity. At the time you had the dream, you were considering taking forty days of your life to put some things aside to seek me in a greater way. You realized that this dream was saying multiplied spiritual prosperity (*2* packs of butter) would come from the forty ($39.99) days you were willing to "pay" or give to me. It was a dream to encourage and direct you in something you were dealing with at that time.

If trying to remember even small, seemingly insignificant dreams are important, an even more vital aspect of valuing dreams is acting upon them. Learn how to apply them to your life in the way they are meant to be applied and then do it. The things I show you are intended for action—prayer, gratitude, changing course or taking some sort of step."

"The things I show you are intended for action."

Dream Backstory: The butter dream came in the wee early stages of my dream education. In addition to the importance of valuing dreams, I had been taught how to better remember them. But, when I tried to recall my dreams from the previous night, all I could remember was that fragment. My conscience wouldn't let it go. After I lifted the dream "crumb" to God as an offering, he multiplied it in front of my eyes. The dream that on the surface seemed to be insignificant and even disappointing to my mind, became a surprising and satisfying meal to my spirit.

$39.99

BUTTER

Not a "Pizza Dream"

"Everyone then who hears these words of mine and does them will be like a wise man who built his house on the rock."

-Jesus, The Bible, Book of Matthew (7:24)

DREAM: Three Factions of People

I saw three factions of people: The first were marine scientists who stayed under the ocean; they were consumed with environmental work including studying whales and dolphins.

The second group lived in caves and were very unfriendly and discontented (the first two groups didn't get along).

The third group was a women's exercise group that met near a river. I was in this group.

In the middle of these groups was a narrow, dark place where Jesus was sitting being ignored. He appeared in a state of having been crucified—no clothes, bloody, sad.

This dream represented three aspects of my life at the time:

#1—The 'environmentalists' represented my obsession with improving my spiritual environment (*water = spiritual matters*). That they were also studying whales and dolphins represented my fixation with following faith leaders or "big fish" and what they said and did.

#2—The grumpy and discontent cave-dwellers represented my attitude toward my hidden and tucked-away life of being a stay-at-home mom.

#3—The women's exercise class represented my attempting to grow and strengthen in relationships. Being near a river represented that I was in line with the flow of God's spirit in that area. Flowing water = God's Spirit, because it is spirit that is *moving*.

The first two groups didn't get along in the dream because those two aspects of my life were incongruent with each other. It didn't make sense that I was trying to improve my spiritual life while being resentful of the physical life God gave me.

And Jesus was in the midst of it all, confined to the tight, little corner in my heart I had allowed for him (*narrow, dark* place). He was waiting for me to stop being indifferent to what he had suffered, and to give him greater space and attention (*ignored, sad*).

Upon this revelation, I knew it was time to turn from my disjointed ways and fix my eyes on the One who had paid the highest price to bring wholeness and order to my life and being.

Ask God to bring to your mind something that has always appealed to you, but you don't know why. Ask him to tell you the story. What is it about that thing, culture, place, person, idea, color, song, etc., that draws or speaks to you? Why?

"" ""

RESOURCEFULNESS IN DREAM SYMBOLS; USING WHAT IS AVAILABLE

"The butter dream brings me to another point. It can be easy to write-off dreams because I will use current life circumstances or experiences to speak to you. Instead of allowing that to get your attention, it is often assumed the dream is the result of the rambling subconscious while the conscious is asleep (a mentality you once identified with, I know).

Like the dream you had when you were in your room with your real-life husband, and he was upset with you for spending $120. That didn't feel very symbolic to you because it was so like reality. But, the specificity of the number 120 caught your attention. You knew that the number 120 in the Bible was the number that would be the limit of a human life. My Spirit revealed to you that this dream was not simply stating the obvious, that your husband did not want you spending excess money. I was telling you through this dream that in spending the money, you were actually spending his life. Your husband trades his very life every day in exchange for income, and that's what you needed to understand.

The $120 was your clue that this dream was symbolic of something more meaningful, in a dream that would have otherwise felt too literal to take seriously. Watch for my clues. I'm always leaving you breadcrumbs, wanting you and helping you to follow the right path.

What's in a Number?

"Watch for my clues."

Dreams like this one are not as "sticky" (sticky as in they linger in your mind and spirit long after you wake up). Most dreams people experience dissipate soon after waking. That is because they are like manna.

My Word tells of how I sent bread from heaven, or *manna*, each day to sustain my children when they were wandering in the desert. But they couldn't gather extra for future days because it wouldn't keep that long. It would go bad after the first day. I did that because I wanted them to learn to rely on me *each day*.

Now, that is not to say that dreams that quickly disappear from your consciousness will "go bad". I'm saying that those dreams are often meant for current situations. The dreams that feel really profound are dreams where I am speaking more clearly for a particular reason. It could be that I'm trying to get your attention or that I am speaking about a much bigger issue. They feel profound because there is a 'weightiness' with that sort of dream; it carries more weight spiritually and therefore an inherently greater weight of responsibility for you.

Those dreams may seem more important, but don't underestimate the power of those small bites of bread that sustain and nourish you between the great feasts. Additionally, there are dreams that you will not be able to remember no matter how hard you try—because I am not allowing you to. That is because your spirit needs the spiritual vitamin but your mind does not. There are certain things that if you knew them would cause harm to you because of your tendency to either get prideful, fearful, or doubtful.

Another reason why a dream may really "stick" to you in waking is because it was real. Real, in the sense that something really happened in the spirit realm. Like the time you were having shoulder pain all night, and you dreamed that your husband grabbed your wrist and wrenched your arm back into socket with a "pop". Your shoulder pain was gone after that, wasn't it? Hahaha!

Think of the possibilities!"

Dream Backstory: My husband is a sole-income provider, and had been for several years prior to having the dream about the $120. He had tried to communicate the weight that comes with independently supporting a family financially, but it was a concept that was difficult for me to fully grasp. This dream was a powerful tool God used to communicate something to my heart that I needed to feel in order to adjust certain behaviors.

Dreams are able to poignantly speak to issues that feel far removed from us and make them feel close in a way that only personal experience usually can. As words from God, they can separate and show the difference between what is soul and spirit, mind and heart.

"The Spirit can *make life*. Sheer muscle and willpower don't make anything happen. Every word I've spoken to you is a Spirit-word, and so it is life-making."

-Jesus, The Bible, Book of John (6:63) MSG

God speaks once, or twice, *yet* no one notices it.
In a dream, a vision of the night, when sound sleep falls on men, while they slumber in their beds, then He opens the ears of men, and seals their instruction, that He may turn man aside from his conduct, and keep man from pride;

-The Bible, Book of Job (33:14-17)

DREAM: Heaven Invading Earth
I went to heaven with my two daughters for a visit. We couldn't see everything. We could only see in part. In fact, all we could see was the color white. My younger daughter saw more than my older daughter. She would run, laughing, with her hand up in the air looking behind her. I knew she was making rainbows with it, but we couldn't see the rainbows.

When we visited the Throne Room, we knew Jesus and the Father were there watching us, though we couldn't see them. They also remained silent, but I could feel their loving approval.

I noticed that what was done on Earth was simultaneously done in Heaven. I also noticed that Heaven and Earth were increasingly getting very close together, to the point where one couldn't tell which one they were in at times.

This was a dream to encourage me in the things I could not see; to know that the realm of Heaven was near, in fact, all around. Also, that God was watching me *and* the next generation (*children*), despite what I see or hear. It was also to show me a greater depth of the connectedness between the actions in the physical realm and the spiritual realm (*what happened on earth simultaneously happened in heaven*).

Rainbows have varied meanings, but one is the *glory* and *multi-faceted nature of God*. This dream showed me the principle that the glory and multi-faceted aspects of God are only seen through childlike faith, since my younger daughter was the only one able to see them.

Notice the two meanings for 'children' in this dream— 'next generation' and 'childlike faith'. Though not the norm, different symbols can have different meanings not only in different dreams, but even in the same one. There are often layers and varying depths of meaning to things of a spiritual nature, and seeking the help of The Spirit is what will draw those layers out.

Gratitude was the only appropriate response for God's willingness to divulge this precious, revealed understanding to me. He didn't have to. Additionally, it encouraged me to be more intentional about my actions and prayers, seeing "with my own eyes" the profound connection between the physical and the spiritual, and to have childlike faith in so doing.

Ask God what your spirit animal is and why. What are the metaphors and symbolism *?*

"" ""

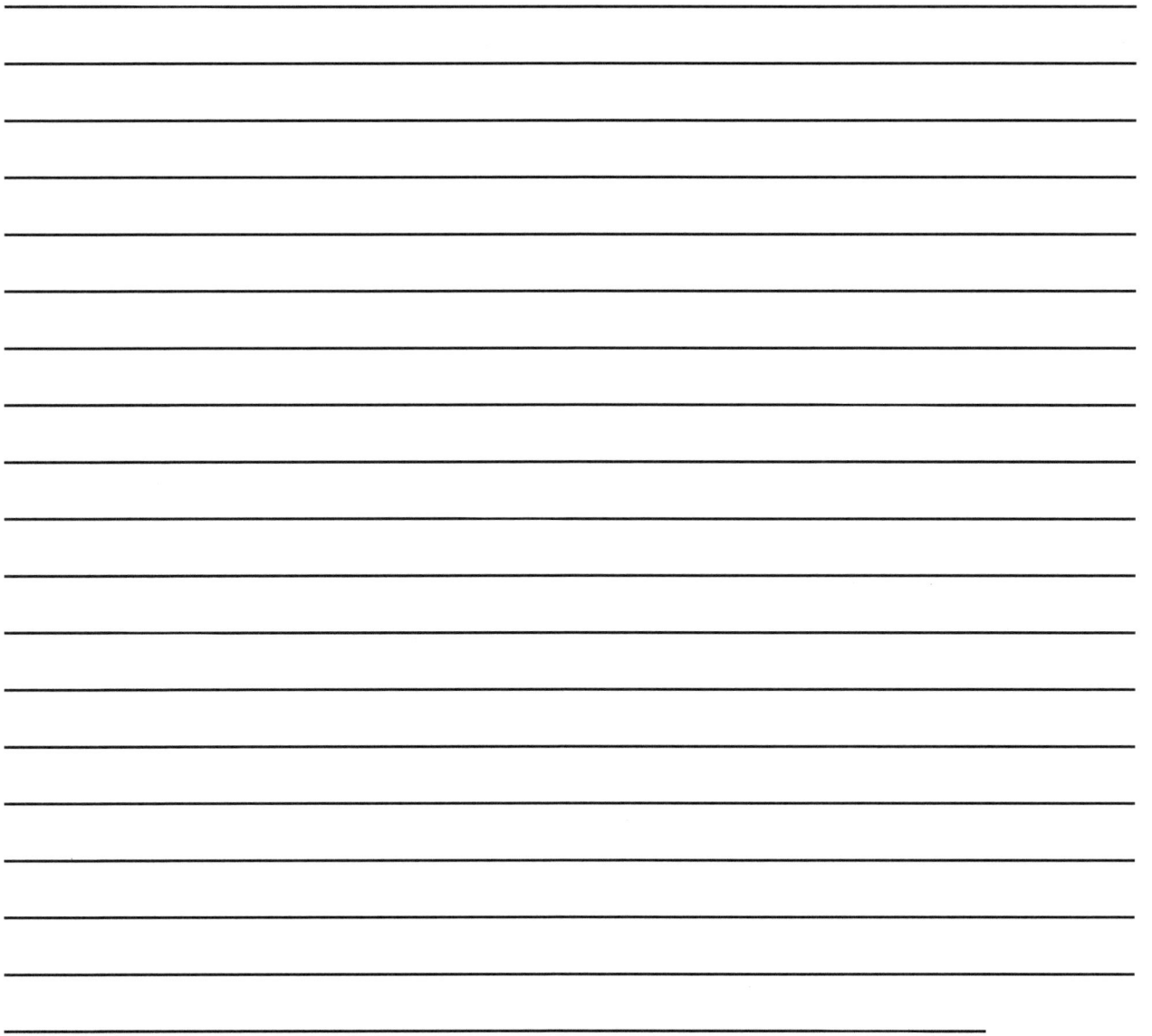

EAT THE MEAT, SPIT OUT THE BONES

"The manna comparison I used to describe dreams is another example of metaphor. It's also an example of a powerful interpretation principle—metaphors are not allegorical. *Everything* doesn't mean *something*.

If you looked at the manna-to-dream comparison allegorically, you would read into everything, therefore thinking harder to remember dreams are useless if you don't interpret them that day. That was not the point being made. It can be easy for my precious analytical, detail-oriented, left-brained people to get tangled up in every detail in metaphors. Not only in meanings of individual symbols, but in the details of the dream as a whole.

You know the saying, "The devil is in the details", right? Well, that's sort of a joke, but also true. Dark forces would love nothing more than to bog your mind down in details so that you lose the overall message; to not see the forest for the trees (which, by the way, is a colloquialism—I use those in dreams along with wordplays and puns—so be watching!).

A helpful thing to do when trying to interpret a confusing or complex dream is to remove the details, stripping it down to its basic plot. Take away the metaphor if you must. Sometimes the context of a symbol matters more than the symbol itself.

For example, instead of saying, "In my dream I went to China," say, "I went to a far place I've never been to," or whatever China would mean *to you*. Symbols are often personal or have unique meaning to each dreamer. China would mean something very different to someone who had never been there versus a resident of the country.

Like the dream where you were going back to school and you were trying to figure out your extracurricular activities. You considered basketball, track, babysitting and dog sitting (the clients of which you didn't have to search for, but came to *you*). All things you had previously done in waking life. You were trying to figure out if you could balance a sport with a job. You instinctively knew basketball wasn't going to work out, so you didn't pursue that activity.

When you went to the track sign-ups it was packed with parents and students. Because of the chaos, you messed up the directions they announced regarding sign-ups. This caused you to miss out on getting a spot on the team. But, by some unexpected miracle you eventually got a spot anyway, and for a position that suited you. Similarly, you had a sense at the end of the dream that somehow things were going to come together.

You could have easily been distracted by, or caught up in all the activities in the dream, but you recognized the big picture. The overall message was saying that of all the things you are considering doing in your life, it's all going to work out. Not because of anything amazing *you've* done, but because I am working behind the scenes. This dream was all about the context of these activities holistically, not as individual elements.

Context is a key way to understand if a suspected meaning for a symbol is right or not, as there can be multiple meanings for any given symbol.

How do you know if something in a dream is a detail (peripheral and not central to the core meaning)? One way is to see if you can remove it and it not change the plot of the dream. Then, you can add that element back into the dream with greater clarity once you understand the main message. But, this is not a rule. Details can also be like the rudder of a ship; small, but pivotal in unlocking a dream's intended purpose. My Spirit whispers these hints to you.

"Context is a key way to understand if a suspected meaning for a symbol is right."

You often wonder how you know what individual symbols mean. Ask yourself what this action, person, place or thing means to you culturally, spiritually or personally. What stands out the most?

If the context around that symbol makes sense and "agrees" with what you're sensing in your spirit, then you know you're on the right track (since we are 'one', your intuition is usually my Spirit speaking to you).

Sometimes certain things are literal in dreams, particularly people or settings. How can you tell if the setting of your dream is literal or symbolic? It's simple—ask!

Context can also give clues. In dreams, if something seems literal as if every aspect about it is like waking life, then it just might be."

Dream Backstory: The dream about the extracurricular activities came at a time where I was in transition, and I didn't know even what that transition would be. I was juggling different directional options and was feeling scattered.

This dream showed me that there may be times when life seems messy or tangled, but there is rest in knowing I don't have to do it all. Nor do I need to feel like I must force things the way I think they need to go. In fact, all I'm ever really doing is putting one foot in front of the other as God guides where it goes.

But he who is joined to the Lord becomes one spirit with Him.

-The Bible, Book of I Corinthians (6:17)

You do not have because you do not ask.

-The Bible, Book of James (4:2)

DREAM: Private School Sneak-In

I was an ethnic boy and I snuck into this private school to become a student. I went on to meet people, made various trips to school and back, went to a football game, gathered notes and did various school-related activities.

I liked the school, but I decided I couldn't afford to go there. But before I could leave, the principal discovered me, confiscated all the notes I had acquired, and kicked me out. At one point, there was a scene where I was a little girl with a group of other little girls and we could fly just by saying a little prayer.

This dream showed me that I was viewing myself as someone on the outside, someone excluded from the privileges and advantages that I saw others have. The fact that it was a private school denoted exclusivity. My conclusion that I couldn't afford it denoted a belief that I wasn't able to do what others were able to do, or go where they were able to go.

In waking life, I knew this was a lie. But, I wasn't acting like it.

God's Spirit revealed to me that if I viewed myself this way, that is how others would view me too. This was exemplified in the dream in how I was kicked out of school.

Furthermore, the notes I had acquired were also taken, which symbolized that what little I had acquired or learned in my attempts to fit in as a self-imposed outsider would not get me anywhere.

That may seem harsh, but that is the ramification of being a poor manager of what we've been given in life, allowing false thoughts and ideas to dictate our action and inaction. You wouldn't choose a doctor for yourself who decided he didn't need to study in medical school, would you? "To those who use well what they are given, even more will be given, and they will have an abundance. But from those who do nothing, even what little they have will be taken away." (Matthew 25:29)

The scene where I was a little girl able to fly was a picture of my true identity. I was meant to be one having childlike faith, able to soar above circumstances (*fly*) with simple acts of spiritual devotion (*simple prayer*). This small scene was in stark contrast with the rest of the dream, where I operated under false pretense.

Therefore, I needed to change my faulty thinking that I didn't belong or I was somehow not worthy, and to see myself the way God did—"above and not beneath". I also needed to be more intentional about making sure I was being faithful with what I had been given and entrusted with in life, even if it didn't feel like very much at the time.

Ask God to take you somewhere of his choosing. Where do you go? Is it past, present, or future? What method do you use to travel? Why that vehicle? Who or what is there? Ask him why he chose that place. Have a conversation with him there. What does this experience tell you about his personality? How can you incorporate this same line of questioning to your dream life?

"" ""

THERE IS NO MORE EXCLUSIVE MEETING PLACE THAN DREAMS

"One of my favorite things to do in dreams is meet with you.

I know you recall the dream where you were on a dock at sunset talking with some people that you knew. Then your husband, Vince, came over—you knew intuitively that he was Jesus.

You had all been discussing with the others whether or not Jesus speaks to you in different ways and you didn't know it. So, you asked him about this when he came over. He gave this coy, playful smile. You took that as a "yes". That was the first time you saw and recognized the playful side of my Son and you relished the encounter. As did I!

Then you gave him a hug and kissed him on the neck. You went on to explain to someone there about a time when you weren't taking in my Word, and you felt your spirit shriveling up like a raisin. Then you explained what it was like when you were finally able to read it again and how your spirit immediately went from a deflated balloon to bursting with life again.

This dream was doing a few things simultaneously. First, it revealed a different side of my Son to you, which is always an impressive and altering experience. Second, it sent the message that I was speaking in ways you weren't discerning, so you could be more receptive. Third, it taught you a principle about the effect my word has on your spirit, how it gives immediate life, simply in the reading. And fourth, it increased your love and value for your husband by using him to represent Jesus. Multitasking, baby!

So, what about the setting? The sunset was letting you know that there was going to be an end of something for you at that time. Water represents things of a spiritual nature, so being on a dock meant that you were hovering on the edge of great things in the spirit realm (since it was a large body of water).

"Seeing a different side of God is always an impressive and altering experience."

Setting Gives Context

There is so much to say on this topic of dreams and our being 'one'; so much that I want to do through it. However, you lack the capacity to absorb it all at one time. That's why, like building a house, I give you a bit more each day.

First, you must have the right foundation to build upon, which is my Word—the Word I have spoken, *and* the Word I continue to speak. Walk with me every day, and I will show you more. I will show you what you need to know, and things you want to know. If you know nothing else about dreams, remember that interpretation based in intellect and logic will fail you. You may get a form of understanding, but never full revelation that changes you and impacts your heart and not just your mind. I am alive. I am active. I am not robotic. I do not speak through formulas. I speak through love.

"I will show you what you need to know."

I hold many keys to your destiny. I want so badly to give them to you. Seek me, and you will find them."

"It takes more than bread to stay alive. It takes a steady stream of words from God's mouth."

-Jesus, The Bible, Book of Matthew (4:4) MSG

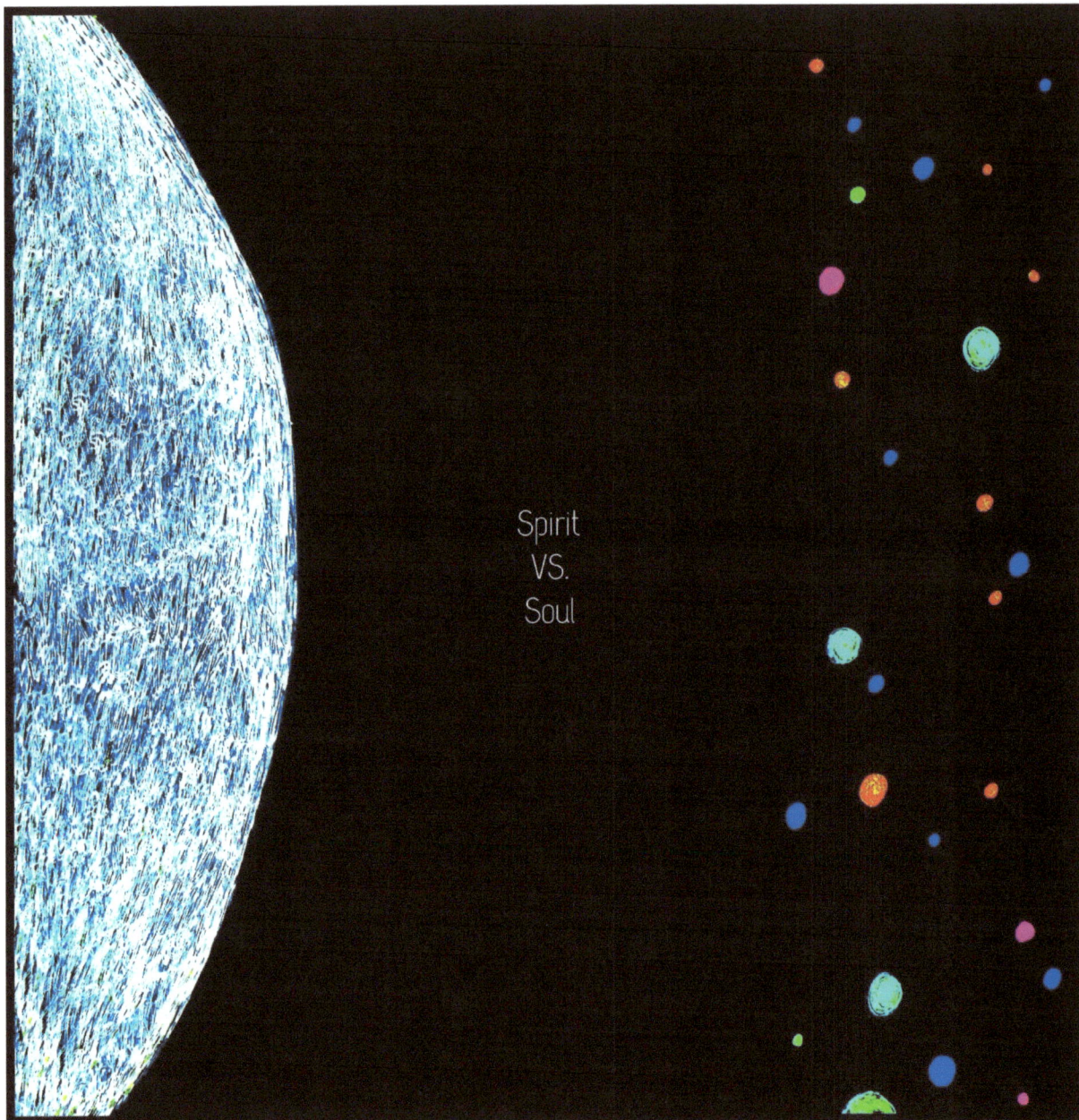

Spirit
VS.
Soul

One Leads, the Other Follows

"I have given you and all my children unique and individual gifts, talents and abilities. I have given them from before you were even conceived, each to help you love me, love others, and be successful in who I've made you to be. But there are also gifts I give throughout your lives.

You will never be able to receive or walk in the fullness of all I have for you if you don't have me, if you don't make room for me in your life and allow me to lead you. Many think that by growing and developing their current potential they are being the best them. But, they have no idea of all they are missing out on by leaving me out. You wouldn't cut a branch off a tree and expect it to go on living, would you? No, of course not. But, that is the way that many people think and live as it relates to me.

Many gifts and abilities are also developed through practice. I can show you the gift. I can teach you how to develop it. I can increase your power in it. I can open doors for you. I can make you see. I can make you hear. I can make you feel. I can make you smell and taste, and in ways and depths you never thought possible. I want to. Call to me, and I will show you things in hidden realms you could never attain on your own."

Dream Backstory: The dream where my husband represented Jesus was very special. Any dream where Jesus chooses to reveal himself is purely amazing (it's interesting how he chooses to reveal himself in manifold ways and in various forms). Christ loves his church the way a husband loves his bride, and that's why it's not unusual for husbands to represent Jesus. In this instance I didn't even have to wonder if that was the case; it was intuitive in the dream.

But, seeing Jesus use my husband to represent himself was something that specifically benefitted me because of the struggles my husband and I had in our marriage. It is a gift to have vision to see your spouse through a more positive light, which this dream did for me. After all, it doesn't get any more positive than Jesus.

"Call to me and I will answer you and tell you great and unsearchable things you do not know."

-God, The Bible, Book of Jeremiah (33:3)

DREAM: Pregnant on a Cliff

My eldest daughter dreamed that we all went to bed and in the morning, I was pregnant. We went to the top of this cliff and I went into labor. I was in a lot of pain. Daddy called the hospital but they couldn't come to help because of the cliff. So, Daddy picked me up and carried me to the hospital and I had a baby girl with yellow hair. She also told me that in the dream I was wearing the same outfit that I was wearing when she was telling me about the dream.

God was showing my daughter something that was going to happen in the future (*clue- I was wearing an outfit in the dream I hadn't worn yet in waking life*).

Being pregnant and going into labor said that what God was developing inside of me was about to be manifested for the world to see on the outside. Since I was suddenly pregnant when we woke up meant that it was going to happen practically overnight, or suddenly.

The fact that I was experiencing labor pain meant that this was going to be a painful process for me. Since it was happening on a cliff and help couldn't reach us meant that it was not going to be something anyone outside of family could help with. My husband carrying me to the hospital meant that my husband alone would be the one able to bear the weight of aiding me through this process.

Yellow is the color of the mind and hope, so this new thing (*baby—a new thing needing attention and care*) would involve those elements.

From this dream experience, I was able to focus on hope during difficult circumstances, knowing that there was great purpose and blessing coming as a result of it. I could be "joyful in hope, patient in affliction."

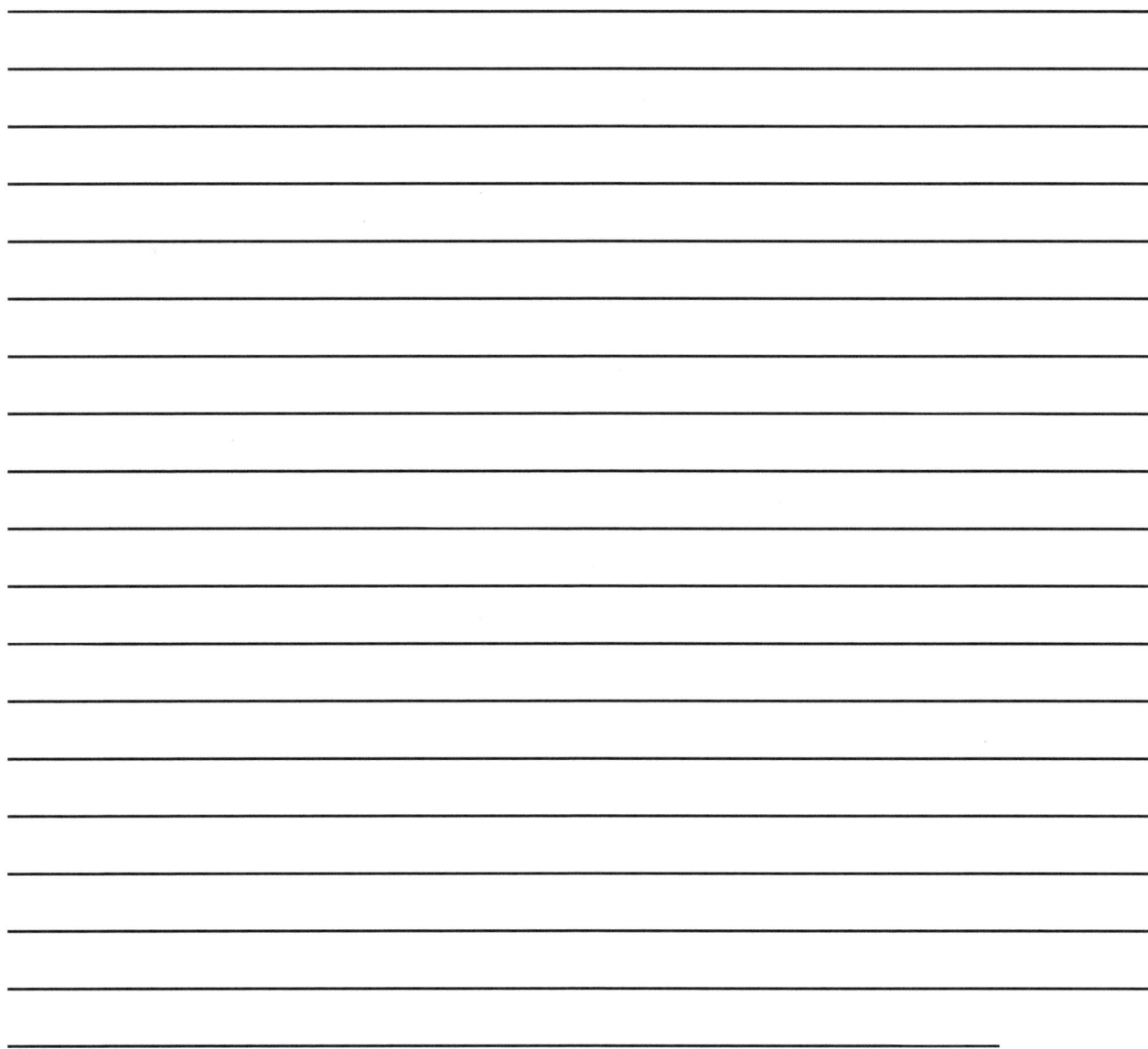

Ask God to bring to your mind something that reminds him of you. What is it?
Ask him why he chose that object or thing. What are the characteristics he
points out? What are the metaphors and symbolism?

"" ""

A PARABLE

"Here is a metaphor for you:

There was a man who was exorbitantly wealthy, kind, intelligent,
captivating, trustworthy, and adoring. He wanted to give his wife, who
made him mad with love, a special gift. He had showered her with
treasures—jewelry befitting royalty, holidays for her and her
companions, love to fill an ocean, as much time and attention as she had
the capacity for. He was even building a home for them to enjoy
together situated cliffside of the most marvelous, pearl-beached vista
that would pale her wildest dreams. He had tailored everything to her
exact tastes and interests, of which, he knew very well.

Still, he had more to give. He was never controlling; never forcing his way; never rough or calloused with her. He had devoted his life to love her, please her and help her grow and blossom as a person. All he ever asked in return was her exclusive love and devotion.

The time for unveiling the vacation home he had worked so hard on was now at hand. He also had a special gift ready for her in his pocket. He was dizzy with anticipation, already picturing the glorious and festive memories with friends and family they would make in their new getaway.

Employing the help of his most trusted friend, the husband went out to seek his wife and bring her to the landing pad where a private helicopter awaited. It was then, they both realized that his wife was nowhere to be found. He checked her favorite reading nook in the garden. He searched the park where she would walk when she needed to gather her thoughts. He checked the art store and the markets she loved to frequent. He returned home and phoned to inquire of her friends. There was no sign of her.

The husband sat at his desk, long past the point of being worried. He looked at the floor, at a loss. Did something happen to her? Why hasn't she come home? Hadn't he done everything he could do to find her? Suddenly, he spotted a scrap of paper adrift on the floor. He picked it up and read a quickly scratched out note from his wife.

She was letting him know that she had left him to go find herself. She wasn't deserving of him, and she needed to find a place in life that seemed more "fitting" for who she was. Furthermore, she had found another man who "didn't require anything of her". A short line at the bottom of the note let him know that she was taking with her the things he had given her and that she may be back one day if she ever needed him.

"Hadn't he done everything he could do?"

Converse Pandora's Box

What do you suppose the wife would find outside of her splendid home? Away from the one who was by far the most devoted and invested in her? Sure, she may find some things that bring temporary satisfaction, but how much more is she going to miss?

The special gift he had been so excited to give her lay next to the note, waiting for the day she would realize that the grass was not greener on the other side. In fact, it wasn't grass at all, but artificial turf. It had the appearance of being beautiful and appealing, but contains no life or growth.

He hoped she would come back before she caused too much harm for herself or before going so far that maybe she would think she *couldn't* come back. He hoped she knew that he would still want her anyway. He was head over heels for her. To her he was wholly committed, but he knew she also had to choose to commit to him too. What good was his commitment without hers?

When that day comes, if ever, the wife would find the ungiven gift to be all the things she went searching for—acceptance, belonging, and an identity that is real and doesn't change according to circumstance.

She would also find that all her desires and every need would be met once again, and the dazzling vacation home he designed through the lens of her every wish was ready and waiting. After all, it was tailored for her. Who else could fill that space in the same way?

So it is with myself and my people. I have given them everything. I will give them everything. They need only to realize that I am their answer. If only they would let me love them and give me their whole heart, I would show them that I can be trusted with it; that I have things for them that only the GREATEST love can give...

Mine.

Now, let me ask you:

You do not limit me by your unbelief, you limit yourself. Are there limits you are erecting around yourself? Is there something you doubt right now?

Is there a way that you have you been like the woman in the story?

Is there anything you are looking for that you think I can't give you? Do you believe that I won't? Why?

What is your perception of me? Of my Son? Of my Spirit? How do those perceptions affect you, for good or bad? Will you let me give you the truth?

Still your mind and heart. Ask me. I will show you."

"Return to me, and I will return to you," says the Lord Almighty.

-The Bible, Book of Malachi (3:7)

"I have swept away your sins like a cloud. I have scattered your offenses like the morning mist. Oh, return to me, for I have paid the price to set you free."

-God, The Bible, Book of Isaiah (44:22)

Allow God to ask *you* a question. What is the first question that comes to you?

What is your answer?

What is his response?

What does this change for you?

AFTERWORD

All the dream examples in this book were real dreams and interpretations given to the author, unless otherwise noted.

Whether you are someone who believes the Bible unquestionably, isn't sure what you believe or does not believe in the authority of the holy Scriptures at all, it is still worth understanding the extraordinary role that dreams play in them. If all the scriptures that involve dreams or visions were added up, they would equal over one-third of the Bible (curious that we also sleep one-third of our lives). That is significant spiritually, historically, culturally and factually. For anyone interested in diving into what the Bible says about dreams with lesson-worthy examples, there is a reference list included.

The Bible says that in the last days, God will pour out his Spirit on *all* people. If you are reading this book, you have no doubt experienced this phenomenon, whether you recognized it as from God or not.

There is a lot of misinformation circulating in the world regarding dreams and spiritual topics. It is my prayer that this book aids as a light exposing counterfeit ideas for what they are; that true enlightenment will be found; that readers will recognize and feel experientially the difference between what is real and what is artificial; between what has a form of power and what has the power to change our lives.

I challenge you today, before closing your eyes in sleep to ask God to give you a dream or vision. Ask him to speak to you. Be open about what he may say and how. His character is predictable, but his methods are far from it. Then, continue the conversation.

ADDITIONAL INFORMATION

These lists are simply to provide some common meanings. As with any symbol in a dream, it's meaning can be personal to the dreamer and can change depending on context. These lists are not meant to be taken as exhaustive or absolute.

Colors:

Red - wisdom, power

Orange - perseverance, caution

Yellow - mind, fear, hope

Green - growth, conscience, money

Light Blue - will, desire

Dark Blue - spirit, revelation

Purple - royalty, authority

Light Pink - childlikeness, immaturity

Dark Pink - emotions, passion

Brown - humility, humanity

Gray - maturity, honor, weakness

Black - evil, darkness

White - righteousness, light

Silver - redemption

Gold - divinity

Multicolor - multi-faceted, glory, promise

Numbers:

1 = Unity, Union

2 = Division, Established/True, Agreement

3 = God (Trinity)

4 = Creativity

5 = Grace (Divine Empowerment)

6 = Humanity, Carnality

7 = Perfection

8 = New Beginning

9 = Journey, Judgement

10 = Completion

11 = Transition

12 = Government

40 = Testing

70 = Generation

Numbers also are often literal. They also can refer to measures of time.

Names:

Aaron– "exalted"

Amanda– "lovable"

Anthony– "priceless"

Christina– "Christian/Christ"

Christopher– "holds name of Christ"

David– "adored, cherished"

Debbie– "Bee"

Elijah– "Jehovah is God"

Elizabeth– "oath or fullness of God"

Erin– "peace"

James– "supplanter, underminer"

John– "love, grace"

Judy– "praise"

Julie– "youthful"

Katie– "pure"

Kendra– "prophetess"

Kyle– "victorious"

Mark– "hammer, shining"

Mary– "bitterness"

Michael– "who is like God?"

Paul– "little"

Peter– "rock"

Ryan– "king"

Samantha– "God hears"

Sarah– "princess"

Thomas– "twin"

Vincent– "conqueror"

Zach– "God remembered"

People can represent various things. If you don't know why a particular person is in your dream and you know their name, find out what their name means. Then see if that meaning fits into the context of the dream.

"We both had dreams," they answered, "but there is no one to interpret them."

Then Joseph said to them, "Do not interpretations belong to God? Tell me your dreams."

-The Bible, Book of Genesis (40:8)

BIBLE REFERENCES

Dreams:

Genesis 20:1-11

    28:10-22

    30:25-43

    31:1-24

    37:1-11

    40-41

Deuteronomy 13:1-3

Judges 7:9-15

1 Kings 3:5-15

Job 33:14-18

Ecclesiastes 5:3

Ezekiel 13:1-7

Daniel *1:17*

    2, 4, 7

Joel 2:28

Matthew 1:18-24

    2:12-15, 19-23

    27:17-26

Visions:

Genesis 15

    46:2-6

Numbers 24:1-14

1 Samuel 3:1-18

2 Samuel 7

Book of Isaiah

Ezekiel 1-3

    43

Daniel *1:17*

    2:19

    8, 9, 10-12

Joel 2:28

Book of Obadiah

Book of Nahum

Habakkuk 2-3

Matthew 17:1-9

Luke 1:5-80

Acts 9:10-18

    10

    16:6-10

    18:9-10

22:17-21
133
7:15-20

2 Corinthians 12:1-4
Proverbs 4:17-19
7:24-27

Book of Revelation
25:2-26:23
9:12-17

Book of Song of Songs
13

Other Metaphor:
Lamentations 1
16:5-12

Judges 9:1-20
Ezekiel 16, 17, 19
20:1-1

2 Samuel 12:1-14
Matthew 5:13-16

Psalm 23
7:3-6

When reading these examples, ask yourself (where applicable):

-What are the metaphoric symbols?

-What do they mean?

-Did you see the connection between the dream/vision/metaphor and its given meaning?

-Where there was a recorded response on the part of the person who the dream/vision/metaphor was for, was it the right response? Did they obey, pray, or share the information with someone? Or did they disobey, get mad, ignore it or have no response at all? What do these examples show you about how to respond to your own dreams and experiences?

"Big Fish"

RESOURCES

Online Classes:

Streams Ministries; John Paul Jackson.
https://www.streamsministries.com/Classroom

> *The Art of Hearing God*

> *Living the Spiritual Life*

> *Understanding Dreams and Visions*

> *Advanced Workshop in Dreams and Visions*

Streams Ministries; John E. Thomas.
https://www.streamsministries.com/Classroom

> *Dream Interpretation Intensive*

Glory Waves; Charity Kayembe. https://www.glorywaves.org

> *Hearing God Through Your Dreams*

Books:

> *The 20 Categories of Dreams Book*; John Paul Jackson and Michael Wise

> *Top 20 Dreams Book*; John Paul Jackson

Understand Your Dreams Now; Doug Addison

Website/Blog:

A Peculiar People; Kelli Rae Hurst. https://www.kelliraehurst.com

-Subscribe on the website and receive the quarterly newsletter on dream interpretation.

The Dream House Training Company. https://www.thedreamhouse.com

Destiny Dreamz. https://www.destinydreamz.com

If you desire more in the way of spiritual hearing exercises, I highly recommend the books:

Rivers from Eden; 40 Days of Intimate Conversations with God by Eden and Brad Jersak. Available at Amazon.com

Cultivating Kingdom Creativity: A Practical Guide to Releasing Supernatural Encounters through Prophetic Arts in Your Personal Life, Church and Community, by Theresa Dedmon. Available at https://shop.bethel.com/

"Psalm 78:2—'I will open my mouth in a parable and utter dark sayings of old.' This verse so describes Kelli Rae's writings and drawings within her books. Kelli, so uniquely in a simple, yet profound way, displays God's wisdom. From creation to the present, her stories tell of God's masterpiece called life, his life he desires to fill us with every day. As you read this book, you will see this life that he came to give you through her writings inspired by her passion."

Paula Sue Thurston,
International Messenger
On *Man of Sorrows*

"The most inspiring, short version of what our Father God did to save human beings, and Jesus' willingness to follow his Father's instructions for us, his creation. This little book should be so easy for children, adults, believers and the lost to understand. It is no mistake with how simply, yet so extensively this plan of salvation was orchestrated between Father and Son in the very beginning…and the amazing hand of the Lord's guidance for Kelli in this work of art!"

Gloria Tissandier
On *Man of Sorrows*

MORE BY THE AUTHOR:

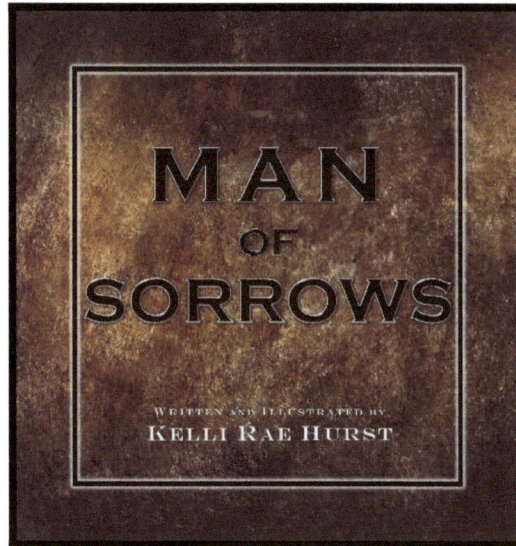

Illustrated. The story of Jesus Christ is infinitely-dimensional. *Man of Sorrows* is a telling which speaks of the sacrifice of Jesus in a way that highlights aspects of his life and suffering often overlooked, glossed over or missed entirely. With a bit of historical context thrown in with the already bountiful knowledge the scriptures offer, the author seeks to amplify the humanity of the person of Jesus, to reveal his accessibility and relatability. He is not fake, unfeeling or far off. He is close. He is relevant. He is brimming with real, authentic and compassionate emotion towards us. He is genuine, he is aware, and he knows what we're going through...from first-hand experience.

If anyone gets us, it's Jesus.

ABOUT THE AUTHOR

Kelli grew up in a Christian family, steeped in a lifestyle in which it was assumed their faith demanded. A set of rules to follow, however, turned out to fall painfully short. She always felt like she was in the dark, on the outside of some great cosmic secret. Early in adulthood, she heeded a voice calling her to embrace and pursue the Truth for herself. That pursuit, ongoing, became the axis of real change.

Now more than a decade later, Kelli has the desire and mandate to empower others with the truths she has learned and experienced by sharing profoundly fundamental principles in a way that is unfiltered, unforced and obtainable.

Kelli is the author of the book, *Man of Sorrows*. She publishes newsletters, personal artwork, and blogs on dream interpretation and more on her website, *A Peculiar People*. www.KelliRaeHurst.com.

Kelli now resides with her husband, Vincent, and their two daughters, Berlin and Petra, in the area of Cincinnati, Ohio.

www.ingramcontent.com/pod-product-compliance
Lightning Source LLC
Chambersburg PA
CBHW061052090426
42740CB00003B/122

* 9 7 8 0 6 9 2 8 8 8 4 7 6 *